Especially for

_____

From

_____

Date

_____

© 2010 by Barbour Publishing, Inc.

Compiled by Todd Hafer in association with Snapdragon Group℠, Tulsa, Oklahoma.

ISBN 978-1-60260-630-2

Published by Barbour Publishing, Inc., P.O. Box 719, Uhrichsville, Ohio 44683, www.barbourbooks.com

Our mission is to publish and distribute inspirational products offering exceptional value and biblical encouragement to the masses.

 Member of the
Evangelical Christian
Publishers Association

Printed in China.

Fun Facts for
Basketball
Fans

BARBOUR
PUBLISHING

When it's played the way it's s'posed to be played, basketball happens in the air; flying, floating, elevated above the floor, levitating the way oppressed peoples of this earth imagine themselves in their dreams.

JOHN EDGAR WIDEMAN

Legendary basketball coach John Wooden was also an accomplished athlete in his day. At Indiana's Martinsville High School, he was a three-time all-state guard who led his team to a state title and two second-place finishes.

Robert Parish is not often mentioned in discussions of the NBA's greatest players, but "The Chief" is the league's all-time leader in games played, with 1,611. Kareem Abdul-Jabbar is second on the list, 51 games back.

During his storied NBA career, Kareem Abdul-Jabbar connected on 15,837 field goals. No one else in league history is close. (Karl Malone is second, with 13,528.)

Adrian Wilson, now a professional athlete—and YouTube sensation—first dunked a basketball at age thirteen, when he was only five feet nine inches tall. Wilson boasts a reported 66-inch vertical jump, which makes him a formidable opponent. . .in the National Football League, where he plays safety. Wilson ultimately chose football over basketball, to the dismay of many NBA scouts and coaches.

Michael Avery, a six foot four inch shooting guard, has accepted a scholarship offer from the University of Kentucky. That's not unusual. However, Kentucky tendered the offer to Avery when he was only a fifteen-year-old eighth grader.

In his rookie year as a pro, Magic Johnson led the Los Angeles Lakers to the NBA title and earned finals MVP honors. However, Johnson was only twenty at the time, making him too young to legally indulge in any of the celebratory locker-room champagne.

Reggie Love, a former college football player who now serves as personal aide to President Barack Obama, has another (unofficial) position in the cabinet. During the president's regular basketball games, he is always teamed with Love. Not only is Love one of the best players on the president's staff, he also serves as "enforcer." Anyone committing a cheap-shot foul on the chief executive risks facing the wrath of Love.

Kobe Bryant scored the 20,000th point of his career when he was only twenty-nine. Bryant is the youngest player to reach the 20,000 mark, besting the great Wilt Chamberlain. By just twelve days.

Despite being a college star at Colorado State University and a four-time WNBA all-star, guard Becky Hammon found herself out in the cold when the U.S. Olympic teams were chosen. So Hammon took a proactive approach. She became a naturalized Russian citizen and competed in the 2008 Olympics. She led the Russians to the bronze medal.

Point guard Jason Kidd has been one of those rare players who have not seen significant depreciation of basketball skills over the years. At age thirty-four, in his fourteenth year in the NBA, he joined Oscar Robertson and Magic Johnson as the only players to average more than 13 points, 9 assists, and 8 rebounds in a single season.

Atlanta Falcons tight end Tony Gonzalez has one of the best "dunk the football over the goal post" celebrations in the NFL. Gonzalez comes by his dunking ability honestly. At the University of California, he was a basketball star as well as a force on the gridiron.

Joe Alexander of the Milwaukee Bucks is one of the best, but least known, dunkers in the NBA.

Alexander is a backup for the Bucks, who see little national television time. Alexander has lobbied to get himself into the annual "Slam Dunk" competition during NBA All-Star Weekend, including creating a Web site called SeeJoeDunk. com. The site shows off Alexander's stunts like holding both arms at his sides and touching the underside of his nose on the rim.

The late Waymon Tisdale had one of the greatest "second acts" in professional sports. After a long NBA career, Tisdale retired to become an award-winning jazz bass guitarist. Even after losing the lower part of his right leg due to a cancerous cyst, Tisdale kept touring in support of his album Rebound, which was inspired by his fight against cancer.

Lost in Tattoo Translation

NBA player Marquis Daniels once thought his Chinese tattoo represented his initials. The tat's actual translation? "Big woman standing on a roof."

Lost in Tattoo Translation, Part 2

NBA veteran Shawn Marion thought his Chinese tattoo meant "Matrix," which is his nickname. The tat's true meaning? "Demon Bird Moth Balls."

Los Angeles Clippers guard Baron Davis showed up for the 2008–2009 season in superb shape, having dropped nineteen pounds from his playing weight of the previous season. The press and Davis's teammates were surprised to learn his secret—a Jenny Craig diet. Davis confessed that his friends teased him, but he countered, "Men should take a page out of a woman's book—because they're smarter than we are."

Observe people who are good at their work—
skilled workers are always in demand and admired;
they don't take a backseat to anyone.

PROVERBS 22:29 MSG

Orlando Magic star Dwight Howard collected his 3,000th career rebound when he was only twenty-one, making him the youngest player ever to reach that milestone.

While in Great Britain for a 2009 preseason game, New Jersey Nets point guard Devin Harris was challenged to a quick game of one-on-one by a young local Brit. Harris lost the game, 2 baskets to none, to the "kid," who is actually a talented street-baller. By the time this book went to press, more than 4.5 million viewers had watched the upset on YouTube.

No player in NBA history was better from the free-throw line than Cleveland's Mark Price. Price's career percentage from the charity stripe stands at .904. No one else has topped 90 percent, though Rick Barry, with his famous underhanded shot, hit an even 90.

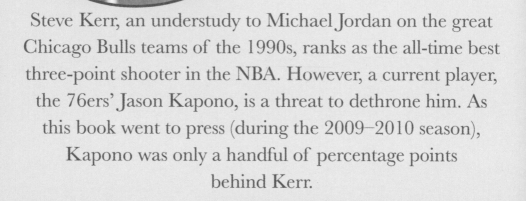

Steve Kerr, an understudy to Michael Jordan on the great Chicago Bulls teams of the 1990s, ranks as the all-time best three-point shooter in the NBA. However, a current player, the 76ers' Jason Kapono, is a threat to dethrone him. As this book went to press (during the 2009–2010 season), Kapono was only a handful of percentage points behind Kerr.

Players with fight never lose a game;
they just run out of time.

COACH JOHN WOODEN

John Stockton, the Hall of Fame guard for the Utah Jazz, never won an NBA championship. However, he is the all-time leader in two key categories. Stockton dished out 15,806 assists during his career, about 5,000 more than second-place Jason Kidd, still active when this book was published. Stockton also grabbed 3,265 career steals, placing him well ahead of No. 2 thief Michael Jordan (2,514).

Boston Celtics guard Rajon Rondo may never be considered as one of the storied franchises all-time greats, but he did his best to etch himself in Boston lore during the 2008–2009 season. His 659 assists and 416 rebounds made him one of only three Celts to post 600 assists and 400 boards in a single season. The other two? Legends Bob Cousy and John Havlicek.

Chicago Bulls rookie Taj Gibson stands a respectable six feet nine, but his outsized arms help him play much bigger than that. His wingspan is seven feet four.

Charlotte Bobcats rookie guard D. J. Augustin sank 89.3 percent of his free throws during the 2008–2009 season. That was the highest total for a rookie since Chris Mullin connected for 89.6 percent back in 1985–1986.

In his 17-year career, Shaquille O'Neal has led the NBA in field-goal percentage nine times. (Incidentally, O'Neal is one of those rare players who regularly fares better from the floor—where he's often double-teamed —than he does from the free-throw line.)

Troy Murphy, who plays center and forward for the Indiana Pacers, is a rare commodity. He is the only player in NBA history to finish in the top 5 in both three-point shooting percentage and rebounding. Murphy achieved this feat in 2008–2009, by hitting 45 percent of his treys and collecting 861 boards in 73 games (an 11.8 per-game average, second-best in the league).

In 2008–2009, Toronto guard Jose Calderon set a new single-season NBA record for free-throw accuracy, hitting 98.1 percent of his shots. He missed only three attempts all season, going 151 for 154.

Omri Casspi, a six feet nine Israeli forward, became the first player from his country to be drafted in the NBA's first round when the Sacramento Kings made him the No. 23 overall pick in 2009. Casspi, who won't turn twenty-two until the 2009–2010 season ends, has been playing pro ball since he was seventeen.

As this book went to press, the San Antonio Spurs were threatening to record the NBA's second-greatest number of consecutive 50-win seasons—with 11. (With a 50-win 2009–2010 campaign, the Spurs will break a tie with the 1958–1968 Boston Celtics, and trail the 1979–91 Lakers, who had 12.)

When coach John Wooden returned home from fighting in World War II, the bank foreclosed on the home he shared with his wife, Nellie. Undaunted, he packed up the family belongings and took a position at Indiana State University. Or, more accurately, several positions. To ensure his family would rebound from financial ruin, Wooden served as ISU's athletic director, head basketball coach, and head baseball coach. He also taught several classes and completed his master's thesis.

Play skillfully with a shout of joy.

PSALM 33:3 NKJV

In 2009, guard Eric Maynor joined the roster of coach Jerry Sloan's Utah Jazz. Twenty-nine years earlier, Eric's father, George, was cut by Sloan, when he was head coach of the Chicago Bulls.

Steals are usually the specialty of crafty guards like John Stockton, Michael Jordan, and Jason Kidd. But the Boston Celtics' all-time leader in the category is Larry Bird, with 1,556. Bird has often been chided for his lack of defensive prowess, but he ranks as the best ball thief in the Celts' 63-year history.

A full regulation basketball game is 48 minutes,
but Golden State's Jamaal Crawford notched 60 minutes
in a 2009 game. (The game went into triple overtime.)

The 1985 NCAA tournament marked the unofficial beginning of "March Madness," as the tourney field was expanded from 53 teams to 64. The tournament was ultimately won by eighth-seeded Villanova, which upset heavily favored Georgetown by hitting 22 of its 28 shots from the floor. This tournament, incidentally, was the last one played without a shot clock.

Retired Utah Jazz forward Karl "The Mailman" Malone, who grew up hunting in Louisiana, is a spokesperson for the National Rifle Association. "About the only thing I'd rather do than play basketball," Malone reveals, "is hunt."

Australia has emerged as a rich place to mine for basketball talent. Thirty-two Aussies dotted 2009 NCAA Division I men's rosters to complement the thirty-nine Aussie women competing at the D-I level. Another one hundred or so hoopsters from Down Under compete at the small-college level.

Milwaukee Buck Andrew Bogut is the most successful
Aussie cager so far. After a great career at the University
of Utah, Bogut was the first overall pick in the
2005 NBA draft.

Minnesota Timberwolves center Kevin Love is the
nephew of Mike Love of the Beach Boys.
However, Kevin, according to a teammate,
"has no singing voice. No rhythm at all."

Phil Jackson, current coach of the Los Angeles Lakers (and formerly of the Chicago Bulls) has led his teams to 10 NBA championships. Two other times, a Jackson team made the finals but finished second. Thus, in 18 campaigns as a head coach, a Phil Jackson squad has been in the NBA finals 12 times.

Star players have an enormous responsibility beyond their statistics. . . . I always thought that the most important measure of how good a game I'd played was how much better I'd made my teammates play.

BILL RUSSELL

Old-school basketball fans might remember that Bill Russell led the Boston Celtics to the 1957 NBA title. But few recall that Russell didn't fully and officially join his team until well into the season that year, mid-January. The reason? He was serving in the U.S. military.

Jerry Sloan has coached the Utah Jazz for the past twenty-two years, the longest tenure in the NBA. Sloan is fourth on the league's all-time wins list with 1,137, and eighteen of his teams have made the playoffs.

One NBA record that is unlikely to be broken is Bill Russell's eleven world titles. Russell's record is even more impressive when one considers that he actually coached himself to the last two championships. (He was a player-coach late in his career.)

Wilt Chamberlain didn't experience an adjustment period while making the transition from the college game to the NBA. He averaged 37.6 points and 27.6 rebounds as a rookie. (For his career, he averaged 30.1 points, 22.9 boards, and 4.4 assists.)

We have a great bunch of outside shooters.
Unfortunately, all our games are played indoors.

WELDON DREW

In 2008, rising star Chris Paul set an NBA record streak of 108 consecutive games with at least one steal. At the other end of the spectrum, current broadcast analyst and former player Scott Hastings has the record for most consecutive games without a steal—with 65.

Bob Pettit of the St. Louis Hawks won the NBA's first-ever Most Valuable Player Award, after a 1955–1956 season in which he led the league in scoring and rebounding.

The 1961–1962 NBA season is one of the most storied campaigns in league history. Wilt Chamberlain averaged 50 points a game, Oscar Robertson averaged a triple-double, and Walt Bellamy averaged 32 points and 19 boards a game. And Bill Russell averaged an incredible 23.6 rebounds a game, yet finished second to Wilt, who averaged 2 boards a game better.

After being named league MVP of the upstart American Basketball Association for his play with the 1969–1970 Denver Rockets, rookie Spencer Haywood bolted for the NBA. One reason? He realized that his purported $450,000 contract with Denver actually paid him only $50,000 a year, then $15,000 annually—after he turned forty.

Wilt Chamberlain once grabbed 55 rebounds in a single game, a record unlikely to be broken. In today's NBA, few teams collectively record 55 boards. And it has been twenty-two years since any player came within 20 rebounds of Wilt's mark. (In 1988, Charles Oakley pulled down 35.)

Elgin Baylor is known as one of the true superstars who retired without winning a championship ring. Baylor's saga is especially poignant. The Laker great retired two weeks into the 1971–1972 season. At that point, the Lakers reeled off 33 straight victories, which propelled them to a 69-win season and an eventual NBA title.

George McGinnis is the king of a dubious category: the turnover. While playing in the ABA in the mid-1970s, he posted the three highest season turnover totals in the history of professional basketball. His totals for those three seasons: 422, 401, and 398— an average of about 5 a game.

Scott Skiles is not regarded as one of the NBA's best-ever point guards. However, he holds the single-game assists record, for dropping 30 dimes in 1990 against the Denver Nuggets. (For comparison, Phoenix's Steve Nash was leading the NBA in assists, with just over 11 a game, when this book went to press.)

"Pistol" Pete Maravich is best known as college basketball's all-time leading scorer. But he was a scoring force in the NBA as well, once notching 68 points in a game—in the era before the three-point bucket. Tapes of Maravich's 68-point effort reveal that at least 7 of his baskets came from beyond the eventual three-point line.

Just a few days before he was to be married to his wife, Nellie, coach John Wooden lost his life savings ($909.05) due to a bank failure. Only a loan from a friend allowed John and Nellie to go through with their wedding.

Rasheed Wallace holds the single-season NBA record for technical fouls, with 41. And Wallace missed five games during the season in which he set the record.

Entering the 2009–2010 season, coach Phil Jackson's teams had won 1,041 of 1,476 games, a .705 winning percentage. And the "Zen Master's" squads have fared almost as well in the playoffs, winning at a 70-percent clip. Jackson's 1996 Chicago Bulls have the all-time single-season wins record, with 72.

Despite forty years in the league—and having LeBron James on the roster for six seasons—the Cleveland Cavaliers have never won an NBA title.

The 1985–1986 version of the Boston Celtics are in the discussion for the best team ever. Led by Larry Bird, the world-champion Celts were especially tough at home. In the oven-like Boston Garden, the green machine went 50–1, including the playoffs.

Forgetting what is behind and straining toward what is ahead, I press on toward the goal to win the prize for which God has called me heavenward in Christ Jesus.

Philippians 3:13–14 NIV

Between 2000 and 2006, Shaquille O'Neal's teams (the Los Angeles Lakers and the Miami Heat) made it to the NBA Finals five times, and O'Neal won three Finals MVP Awards.

Atlanta Hawks guard/forward Josh "J-Smoove" Smith, who entered the NBA out of high school, is the fastest player in league history to reach the 800 blocked-shot mark.

Guard Mike James, currently with the Washington Wizards, has played for 8 teams in 10 seasons in the NBA.

Even Wilt Chamberlain had to look up at the collegiate scoring record. On February 2, 1954, Rio Grande's Clarence "Bevo" Francis poured in 113 points against Hillsdale.

Denver Nuggets point guard Chauncey Billups knows
his city better than most NBA players. He was a star at
Denver's George Washington High School and played his
college ball at the University of Colorado in Boulder,
just a half hour away from Denver.

Me shooting 40 percent from the foul line is just
God's way to say nobody's perfect.

SHAQUILLE O'NEAL

While Jose Calderon is the NBA's best single-season free-throw shooter, Larry Bird has the highest percentage among players with at least 300 attempts (93 percent) and at least 400 (91 percent).

When the NBA introduced the three-point basket, in 1979–1980, players were hesitant to launch shots behind the arc. Only two players, Brian Taylor (with 239) and Rick Barry (221) attempted more than 200 threes over the course of the season.

After winning the NBA title in 1984, the Boston Celtics seemed poised to repeat in 1985. However, Celts superstar Larry Bird injured his shooting hand in a bar fight, and the Magic Johnson–led Los Angeles Lakers beat Boston in the finals. (Bird sustained the injury between Games 2 and 3 of the Eastern Conference Finals, punching out a bartender. His shooting percentage dropped 12 points after the incident.)

Prior to the 1984 Summer Olympics, Bobby Knight cut the following players from the U.S. basketball team: Charles Barkley, Karl Malone, John Stockton, Joe Dumars, and Terry Porter. (Players who made the team include Jeff Turner, Joe Kleine, Steve Alford, and Jon Koncak. And, oh yeah, Michael Jordan.)

In the 1984 draft, the Portland Trail Blazers chose center Sam Bowie over Michael Jordan. That left Jordan on the board when it was time for the Chicago Bulls to make their choice.

Cynthia Cooper was the WNBA's first superstar. In the league's first four years, Cooper led her Houston Comets to the championship each time. Her feat is even more impressive when one considers that "Coop" was thirty-three when her WNBA career began. (Before the league's formation, she spent eleven years playing pro ball in Europe.)

Los Angeles Laker Elgin Baylor was a U.S. Army Reservist during six months of the 1961–1962 season. This meant that he lived in army barracks during the week, then flew (coach class), when he had a weekend pass, to join the Lakers wherever they were playing. He averaged 38 points and 19 rebounds for the season.

During the 2001–2002 season, Jason Kidd dove into the stands for a loose ball. Unfortunately, he landed on his young son and broke his collarbone.

After Moses Malone made basketball history by jumping straight from high school to the pros, fourteen years passed before another high schooler thrived in the NBA. Shawn Kemp became a solid member of the Seattle Supersonics, although a potential Hall of Fame career was undermined by boorish on-court behavior and a multitude of off-the-court problems.

Discipline isn't much fun. It always feels like it's going against the grain. Later, of course, it pays off handsomely, for it's the well-trained who find themselves mature in their relationship with God.

HEBREWS 12:11 MSG

All-Stars Chris Mullin and Magic Johnson guarded each other for Game 2 of the 1991 playoff series between Mullin's Golden State Warriors and Johnson's Lakers. "Guarded" is a relative term. Magic scored 44 points, and Mullin 40. Golden State won the game, 125–124.

The Orlando Magic fired head coach Brian Hill in 1997. The Vancouver Grizzlies then hired Hill, who posted an anemic 31–123 record. Thus, the Grizzlies fired Hill in 2000. Five years later, Hill was hired as a head coach again. His "new" employer: The Orlando Magic.

On April 9, 1978, Denver's David Thompson scored 32 points in one quarter, a new NBA record, on the way to a halftime total of 53. For the first time in years, Wilt the Stilt's 100-point record looked reachable. However, Thompson ended up with 73. (And, five hours later, San Antonio's George Gervin scored 33 in one quarter, making Thompson's record one of the most short-lived in NBA history.)

The 1992 Detroit Pistons averaged 44.3 rebounds a game. Dennis Rodman accounted for 42 percent of that total. For comparison, Bill Russell's highest rebound percentage for one season was 35. Wilt's highest was 37 percent.

Paul Arizin, one of the NBA's stars of the 1950s, was the first player to employ a jump shot instead of a set shot. Arizin was the first player to average 20 plus points for 9 straight seasons, despite chronic sinus problems that hampered his ability to run the court.

Tommy Heinsohn was so gifted and so smart that if he'd made up his mind to play every night, the only forward who would have been any competition was [Elgin] Baylor. Not even Pettit could have come close to him.

BILL RUSSELL, on his prank-playing, hard-partying Celtics teammate

In the playoffs, no player has been better than Bill Sharman from the free-throw line. Among those with at least 75 post-season games, no one can top Sharman's career 91.1 percent accuracy.

Chicago Bull James Johnson, the sixteenth pick in the 2009 draft, was undefeated as a kickboxer before his basketball career took off.

Clair Bee, who coached the Long Island University Blackbirds from the 1930s to the 1950s, went on to become a successful novelist. Bee is the creator of the Chip Hilton sports fiction series.

The record for consecutive free throws is held by seventy-one-year-old Tom Amberry, who sunk 2,750 of them. Incidentally, Amberry didn't miss his 2,751st shot; he merely got tired of shooting and headed off for dinner.

The 1960 U.S. Olympic team, captained by recent college grads Oscar Robertson and Jerry West, easily won the gold medal. The Americans flattened their eight opponents by an average of 42 points.

LeBron James was not the first high school basketball star to grace the cover of *Sports Illustrated* magazine (in 2002). Rick Mount was the first prep cover boy in 1966, and he was followed by Tom McMillen, Mike Peterson, and Kevin Garnett.

James Naismith devised his "13 precepts of basketball" in 1891. Naismith created the game to help win over a restless class at a YMCA training school. The first baskets were aptly named—peach baskets, with the bottoms still in them.

In March 1893, just fifteen months after basketball was invented, the first women's game was played at Smith College.

Langston University thoroughly enjoyed its reign during superstar Marques Haynes's collegiate years. Haynes led the team to a 112–3 record. One of those wins was against the famed Harlem Globetrotters, whom Haynes would one day join as a player.

Left hand, right hand, it doesn't matter.
I'm amphibious.

CHARLES SHACKLEFORD

Wilt Chamberlain is best known as a scorer and a rebounder. However, in 1968, while playing for Philadelphia, the seven-footer led the NBA in assists.

In a late-November game in 1950, the Fort Wayne Pistons helped set a record for offensive futility. The Pistons managed only 19 points in the game. Fortunately, their opponents, the Minneapolis Lakers, scored 18.

Wilt Chamberlain scored his record 100 points in a 169–147 victory for his Philadelphia Warriors over the New York Knicks. A sparse crowd of 4,124 watched the Stilt make 36 of 63 field goals and 28 of 32 free throws.

During the decade of the 1960s, the Boston Celtics won an astounding 9 NBA championships. Those Celtic teams featured the likes of Bill Russell, Tommy Heinsohn, John Havlicek, and Bob Cousy.

Pete Maravich was a legendary scoring machine in college. In his three seasons at LSU (freshmen were not allowed to play varsity ball in Pistol Pete's era), he averaged 43.8, 44.2, and 44.5 points a game, in the era before the three-point basket. He posted at least nine 50-point games each season.

Yao Ming is tall (seven feet six inches), but even he would have to gaze upward to Libya's Suleiman Ali Nashnush. Nashnush stood eight feet, making him the tallest player in organized basketball history.

NBA star Bill Sharman was also a fine baseball player. He played third base in the Brooklyn Dodgers farm system in the early 1950s. He was called up to the majors in 1951, but was thrown out of his only big-league game for yelling at an umpire—from the dugout—before he had actually appeared in on the field. Undaunted, he continued to moonlight as a minor league player during the early years of his NBA career.

I'll tell you this; you did not drive by [Bill Sharman].
He got into more fights than Mike Tyson.

JERRY WEST

In 1943, a friend gave coach John Wooden a small wooden cross, which he carried in his pocket from that moment on. "I held it in my hand during games, during times of tension. It reminded me who is in control," Wooden explained. "It probably is a good thing for officials that I had that cross in my hand when a bad call was made."

At the time Wilt Chamberlain scored his historic 100 points (in March of 1962), he also had the season's No. 2 and No. 3 top-scoring games. In a January game, he scored 73 points, in regulation. About a month before that, the Stilt exploded for 78 in a triple-overtime contest.

From 1957 to 1969, the Boston Celtics won 11 NBA titles in 13 seasons. At one point (from 1959), the Celts ran off 8 consecutive championships, a feat unlikely to be equaled.

After John Havlicek's steal preserved the Boston Celtics'
victory in the 1965 Eastern Division finals, the Celts'
rabid fans stormed the court and lifted "Hondo"
on their shoulders. In the process, they tore
his jersey off his body.

I haven't been able to slam-dunk the basketball for the past five years. Or for the thirty-eight years before that, either.

DAVE BARRY

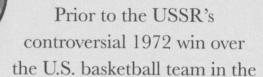

Prior to the USSR's controversial 1972 win over the U.S. basketball team in the finals of the 1972 Olympics, the Americans had won seven straight gold medals. The U.S. team was so upset over the loss that they declined receiving the silver medals.

To this day, the medals remain in a vault in Switzerland, and will be claimed only in the unlikely event that the entire U.S. team agrees, unanimously, to accept them. (Don't hold your breath.)

Despite a torn thigh muscle, New York Knicks center Willis Reed insisted on playing in Game 7 of the 1970 NBA Finals, against the Los Angeles Lakers. Reed scored only 2 baskets in the game, but they were on the Knicks' first 2 possessions, and they set the tone for the game. More important was Reed's tough defense against Wilt Chamberlain, the key in the Knicks' 113–99 win.

At Purdue University, future Hall of Fame coach John Wooden was a three-time All-America guard who led the Boilermakers to a pair of Big Ten titles and the 1932 national championship. Wooden also lettered in baseball at Purdue—as a freshman.

Be on your guard; stand firm in the faith;
be men of courage; be strong.
Do everything in love.

1 Corinthians 16:13–14 NIV

The 1979 NCAA Championship game between Indiana State and Michigan State received the highest Nielsen television rating ever for a collegiate tournament game. The contest itself lacked drama, however, as MSU's match-up zone defense frustrated ISU's Larry Bird. Magic Johnson's Spartans held a double-digit lead for most of the game and won 75–64. (Bird finished with 19 points, on 7 of 21 shooting.)

Entering the 1983 NCAA basketball tournament, the North Carolina State Wolfpack carried ten losses on its record. But the Pack clawed its way to the championship game, against top-ranked Houston. Then, with its 54–52 last-second victory, Coach Jim Valvano's team became NCAA champions, despite suffering the most regular-season losses of any championship squad.

In a game against the Utah Jazz, Boston's Larry Bird posted a triple-double and 9 steals in just 33 minutes of playing time. Before the game's fourth quarter, Boston coach K.C. Jones offered to put Bird in the game so that he could secure the rare quadruple-double. But since Boston had the game well in hand, Bird declined and sat out the entire quarter.

The fifth game of the 1997 NBA Finals found Chicago Bulls superstar Michael Jordan suffering from a severe case of the flu—or food poisoning, depending on whether you believe in conspiracy theories. But Jordan insisted on playing. Several times near the end of the game, he came close to passing out. When he won the game for his team, with his 38th point, he could no longer stand. His teammates had to prop him up, even while he was seated on the bench.

Michael Jordan, who would go on to win 6 NBA championships, was cut from his Wilmington, North Carolina, high school basketball team, as a sophomore. (He mentioned the perceived slight in his 2009 Hall of Fame acceptance speech.)

Michael Jordan averaged 28.2 points his rookie year in the NBA, and was an All-Star Game starter and Rookie of the Year. However, some basketball fans don't recall that it took Jordan seven NBA seasons before his Chicago Bulls won their first world title.

In 1994, after Michael Jordan retired from basketball (for the first time), he played baseball for the Birmingham Barons, a class AA farm team for the Chicago White Sox. The best-known minor league outfielder in the country, Jordan hit a respectable .259 during his last month of the season, ending up with 50 RBIs and 30 stolen bases. (He would return to the NBA in the middle of the 1995 season.)

Any young kid who plays basketball at a playground in the Los Angeles area just might have actor/philanthropist Kirk Douglas to thank. Douglas and his wife, Anne, began rebuilding playgrounds in the late 1990s, when the actor was 80. He dedicated his 401st playground eleven years later.

At age fifty, Nancy Lieberman came out of retirement to sign a seven-day contract with the WNBA's Detroit Shock. She dished out 2 assists in 9 minutes in a game against the Houston Comets, then retired as the oldest player to take the floor in league history.

Irma Garcia is one of those people who can claim true loyalty to her school. She played basketball for St. Francis College, and then served as a coach. Later, at age forty-nine, she became the school's athletic director, making her the first Hispanic to serve in such a position at a Division I school.

In a 1972 game, West Coast Christian College led the University of California at Santa Cruz by 13, with just over 2 minutes in the game. However, a series of foul-outs had rendered WCCC with just one player, guard Mike Lockhart. Lockhart, who had four fouls himself, gamely battled five opponents and was outscored only 10–5 for the contest's remaining time. His Knights beat the Sea Lions 75–67.

In a 1925 girls' game, Fargo, North Dakota's, Kensal High School and Pingree High School finished regulation play in a 0–0 tie. The game spilled over to three overtimes—with the teams still locked in a scoreless tie. The coaches and referees, seeing the handwriting on the wall, eschewed a fourth overtime and flipped a coin to determine the winner. Kensal's coach correctly called "Heads" and Pingree went home, a 0–0 loser.

The All-Wall Street Team
(G) Phil Bond
(G) Mark Price
(C) Laron Profit
(F) Eric Money
(F) Gene Banks

Longtime college hoops fans know that Michigan State won the 1979 NCAA title, as Magic Johnson's Spartans defeated Larry Bird's Indiana State Sycamores. However, most people don't know that eight games into its Big Ten Conference schedule, the Spartans were only 4–4, including a humiliating 18-point loss to Northwestern, the conference's worst team. ISU, on the other hand, was undefeated going into the championship game.

"Pistol" Pete Maravich is Division I college basketball's all-time leading scorer, with a career average of 44.2 points. Maravich set his record in the era before the three-point basket. After reviewing game footage, basketball historians have calculated Maravich's potential scoring average, had he been credited with treys. The result: 57 points a game.

The NBA logo is modeled after former Los Angeles great Jerry West. The Laker guard was a fourteen-time NBA All-Star.

From January of 1971 to January 1974, Coach John Wooden's UCLA Bruins won 88 consecutive games, an NCAA record that will probably never be broken.

"Take courage! Do not let your hands be weak,
for your work shall be rewarded."

2 CHRONICLES 15:7 NRSV

The 1972–1973 Philadelphia 76ers finished the season with fewer than 10 wins (9–73). That's a winning percentage of only 11—an NBA worst.

Larry Bird is not the only successful basketball-playing "Bird." In 1973, Pepperdine University's Bird Averitt led the NCAA in scoring, averaging 33.9 points a game.

Portland State's Freeman Williams scored at least
66 points three different times during his career.
He led the NCAA in scoring in 1977
(38.8 points a game) and 1978 (35.9).

The size-22 shiny red "Dunkman" sneakers that Shaq O'Neal wore during the 2004 season are the largest in NBA history. (Shaq's shoes are the largest in terms of mass; Hall of Fame center Bob Lanier wore a shoe that was actually longer.)

Houston Rockets center Hakeem Olajuwon was a dedicated Muslim, as well as a fine player. He was so devout in his faith that he observed calorie-depleting ritual fasts even during the playoffs.

DePaul's Ray Meyer recorded one of the most impressive coaching tenures in any sport. Meyer coached the Blue Demons for forty-two seasons. One of his protégés was George Mikan, who went on to become the NBA's first dominant big man.

I never encouraged anyone to pray for a win. I don't think our prayers should be directed to the score of a game. That seems way too selfish. I wanted my boys to honor God by doing their best, controlling their emotions, and asking for protection.

COACH JOHN WOODEN

In 2007, the University of Florida simultaneously held two national titles, in football and basketball. No other Division I school has managed this feat. Ironically, the Gators beat Ohio State in the title games on the gridiron and the hardwood.

Despite standing only five feet five, guard Earl Boykins was a solid player at Eastern Michigan, then in the NBA, where he is one of the league's top foul shooters. But Boykins is not the NBA's most diminutive player. That title goes to five feet three Muggsy Bogues.

During the 2009–2010 NBA season, Kobe Bryant earned membership in yet another elite club. With his 100th 40-point game, he joined Wilt Chamberlain and Michael Jordan in the three-person 100/40 Club.

Bill Russell is well known for his eleven NBA titles. But the talented center also won two NCAA titles and an Olympic gold medal.

The only difference between a good shot
and a bad shot is if it goes in or not.

CHARLES BARKLEY

One of the attractions at the Basketball Hall of Fame in Springfield, Massachusetts is the pair of floppy gray socks that LSU's Pete Maravich wore the night he scored 69 points against the University of Alabama.

Coach Bobby Knight's 1975–1976 Indiana Hoosiers battled to a perfect 32–0 season and won the NCAA Championship. The Hoosiers went wire-to-wire as the nation's top-ranked team. They opened the season against defending champion UCLA and beat ninth-ranked Michigan—for the third time—in the championship game.

One of all-star guard John Stockton's secret weapons as a player was his cardiovascular fitness. During his playing days, his resting heart rate was in the midthirties, a similar number to elite marathon runners and distance cyclists. (The average man's resting heart rate is seventy-two beats per minute.)

During the twilight of his playing days, Indiana Pacer George McGinnis could sometimes be found on the end of the team bench, smoking a cigarette.

In a 1997 game, the Dallas Mavericks'
Bubba Wells fouled out in just 3 minutes—
the fastest disqualification in NBA history.

The invention of basketball was not an accident. It was developed to meet a need. Those boys simply would not play "Drop the Handkerchief."

DR. JAMES NAISMITH

I never yelled at my players much. That would have been artificial stimulation, which doesn't last very long. I think it's like love and passion. Passion won't last as long as love. When you are dependent on passion, you need more and more of it to make it work. It's the same with yelling.

COACH JOHN WOODEN

NBA All-Boating Team
(G) Danny Ferry
(F/G) Joakim Noah
(C) Eddie Mast
(F) Curtis Rowe
(F) Louis Orr

All-American Revolution Team
(G) World B. Free
(G/F) Alex English
(C) George Washington
(F) Marcus Liberty
(F) Keith Starr

All-Second-Career Team

(G) Bill Bradley (U.S. senator, author,
and presidential candidate)

(G) Chuck Conners (actor—*The Rifleman*)

(C) Tom McMillan (U.S. congressman)

(F) Wayman Tisdale (jazz musician)

(F) Mark Hendrickson (major league baseball player)

All-The President's Men Team
(G) Norm Nixon
(G) Earl Monroe
(C) George Washington
(F) Gene Kennedy
(F) Garfield Heard

All-The President's Men Team, Version 2.0
(G) T. J. Ford
(G) Gary Grant
(C) Roosevelt Bowie
(F) Vince Carter
(F) Richard Jefferson

Morningside High School's Lisa Leslie once scored 101 points in the first half of a game. Cheryl Miller's all-time prep record of 105 seemed easily within Leslie's grasp. Unfortunately, Morningside was walloping its opponent so badly that the game was forfeited at halftime, and Miller hung on to the record.

A.C. Green holds the record for most consecutive games played, with 1,192. Green began the streak in 1986. It ended in 2001, when he retired.

In a 1997 college contest, Long Island beat Medgar Evers by 117 points, the most lopsided victory in collegiate history.

When the United States Olympic "Dream Team" blew out Croatia 117–85 to win the 1992 gold medal, it was the smallest margin of victory for a contingent that included Michael Jordan, Larry Bird, Charles Barkley, and Magic Johnson. (The Dream Team was assembled in response to the United States' shocking and disappointing third-place finish at the '88 Olympics.)

In the 1993 NCAA championship game, Texas Tech's Sheryl Swoopes scored more than half (47) of her team's points in an 84–82 win over Ohio State. Swoopes's total remains a points record for an NCAA title game.

In 1988, diminutive New York Knicks coach Jeff Van Gundy tried to break up a brawl between members of his team and the Miami Heat by attaching himself to the lower left leg of Miami's Alonzo Mourning and hanging on for dear life.

Tell me I play like a man, and I'll tell you, "Hey, thanks."
The best players in the world are men,
so why wouldn't you want to play like them?

COLLEGIATE AND WNBA STAR DIANA TAURASI

U.S. President Gerald Ford could have played professional football had he not entered the navy after college. But he was also a fine basketball player, with decent hops. He was known to demonstrate his hoops skills in shirts versus skins games aboard the USS *Monterey*.

In the 1984–1985 season, Utah's Mark Eaton averaged 5.56 blocked shots per game, an NBA record. Eaton's seven feet four height was a factor in his success, but he also possessed great defensive timing and an instinct for being in the right place at the right time.

After watching the likes of Darryl Dawkins and Jerome Lane shatter backboards with their thundering dunks, Illinois farmer Arthur Ehrat created a breakaway rim, featuring a heavy-duty coil spring from a John Deere cultivator. Ehrat was granted a 1982 patent for his invention, which has reduced injuries and the number of game delays and postponements at all levels of basketball.

Throughout the entire decade of the 1960s, the NBA was led in rebounding each season by either Bill Russell or Wilt Chamberlain. (Wilt was chairman of the boards 8 times, to complement his 7 scoring titles.)

The five people who first come to mind that best reflect the quality of integrity are Jesus, my dad, Abraham Lincoln, Mother Teresa, and Billy Graham. The order of the last three really doesn't matter.

COACH JOHN WOODEN

In the NBA's highest-scoring game of all time, a 186–184 Detroit Pistons' win over the Denver Nuggets, four players scored more than 40 points. Topping the 40-point mark in the triple-overtime contest were Denver's Kiki Vandeweghe (51) and Alex English (47) and Detroit's Isiah Thomas (47) and John Long (41).

NBA All-Kitchen Team
(G) Spud Webb
(G) Vinnie "Microwave" Johnson
(C) Mel "Dinner Bell Me!" Turpin
(F) Cornbread Maxwell
(F) Brian "Veal" Scalabrine

[John Havlicek] is the best all-around player I ever saw.

BILL RUSSELL

In its rankings of "All-Time, All-Size All-Stars," *Sports Illustrated* magazine chose Ann Meyers as the best five foot eight inch player of all time, ahead of male players like Charlie Criss.

Legendary Celtics coach Red Auerbach held the firm belief that referees were biased against him. He was known to berate officials even when their calls went Boston's way. Once, he started an argument with referee Sid Borgia in the lobby of the Boston Garden. The argument soon escalated to a full-on fistfight.

Bob McAdoo of the Buffalo Braves led the NBA in scoring for three straight seasons. He averaged 30.6 points a game in 1974, 34.5 in 1975, and 31.1 in 1976. (McAdoo's streak was broken by Pete Maravich of the New Orleans Jazz, who finished the 1977 season with a league-leading 31.1.)

In 1940, during basketball's "barnstorming" days, a
reserved ticket for a game between the world champion
"Original Celtics" (coached and captained by the legendary
Joe Lapchick) and the Mercer Ramblers
went for a dollar and a half.

One doesn't necessarily need to average big points to enjoy longevity in the NBA. Seven foot five inch Chuck Nevitt played 155 games in a 9-year NBA career, with 5 different teams. His career scoring average: 1.6 points a game.

The 1986 NBA slam dunk competition was won by Atlanta's Spud Webb, owner of a 46-inch vertical leap. Webb's official height: five feet seven inches.

Julius is the most exciting player I've ever seen. He'll keep people in the arena until the 48th minute, because they're afraid if they leave he might do something nobody's ever seen before—or ever will again.

BASKETBALL EXECUTIVE CARL SCHEER, on Julius "Dr. J" Erving

In leading Duke to its epic NCAA tournament victory over Kentucky in 1992, Christian Laettner was perfect from the floor (10 for 10) and the free-throw line (also 10 for 10). Laettner's last-second basket marked the game's fifth lead change in the final 31.5 seconds. For the game, the teams shot a combined 61 percent.

Identical twins Tom and Dick Van Arsdale starred on the 1962 Indiana University team. The twins were so identical that they scored almost the same amount of points for the season, with Tom edging his brother by just 12 points.

Center Artis Gilmore led both the ABA and the NBA in field-goal percentage. (Gilmore is one of the ABA players who survived the NBA's absorbing its rival league.)

Even though his Purdue team didn't reach the championship game, Bill Bradley was named 1965 NCAA Tournament MVP. In the third place game, Bradley poured in 58 points to lead the Boilermakers to a 118–82 win over Wichita State. Bradley's mark is still a Final Four scoring record.

Wilt Chamberlain would not have scored his historic 100 points without an uncharacteristically good night from the charity stripe. Normally only a 51 percent free-throw shooter, Chamberlain hit 28 of his 32 shots (87.5 percent) on his record-breaking night in Hershey, Pennsylvania.

In 1960, the United States was still using only amateur players on its Olympic teams. But that squad was one impressive collection of amateurs. The U.S. team featured future pros Jerry Lucas, Jerry West, Oscar Robertson, and Walt Bellamy—who dominated Brazil 90–63 in the gold medal game.

The All-Geography Team
(G) Brad Holland
(G) Michael Jordan
(C) Mike Brittain
(F) Ken Spain
(F) Kendall Rhine

The All-Navy Team
(G) Darrell Carrier
(G) John Battle
(C) Charlie Shipp
(F) Terry Furlow
(F) Kenny Sailors

Larry Kenon is arguably the least-known player to hold an NBA single-game record. Kenon once recorded 11 steals.

Strengthen the weak hands, and make firm the feeble knees. Say to those who are of a fearful heart, "Be strong, do not fear!"

ISAIAH 35:3–4 NRSV